Master Class
Juggling

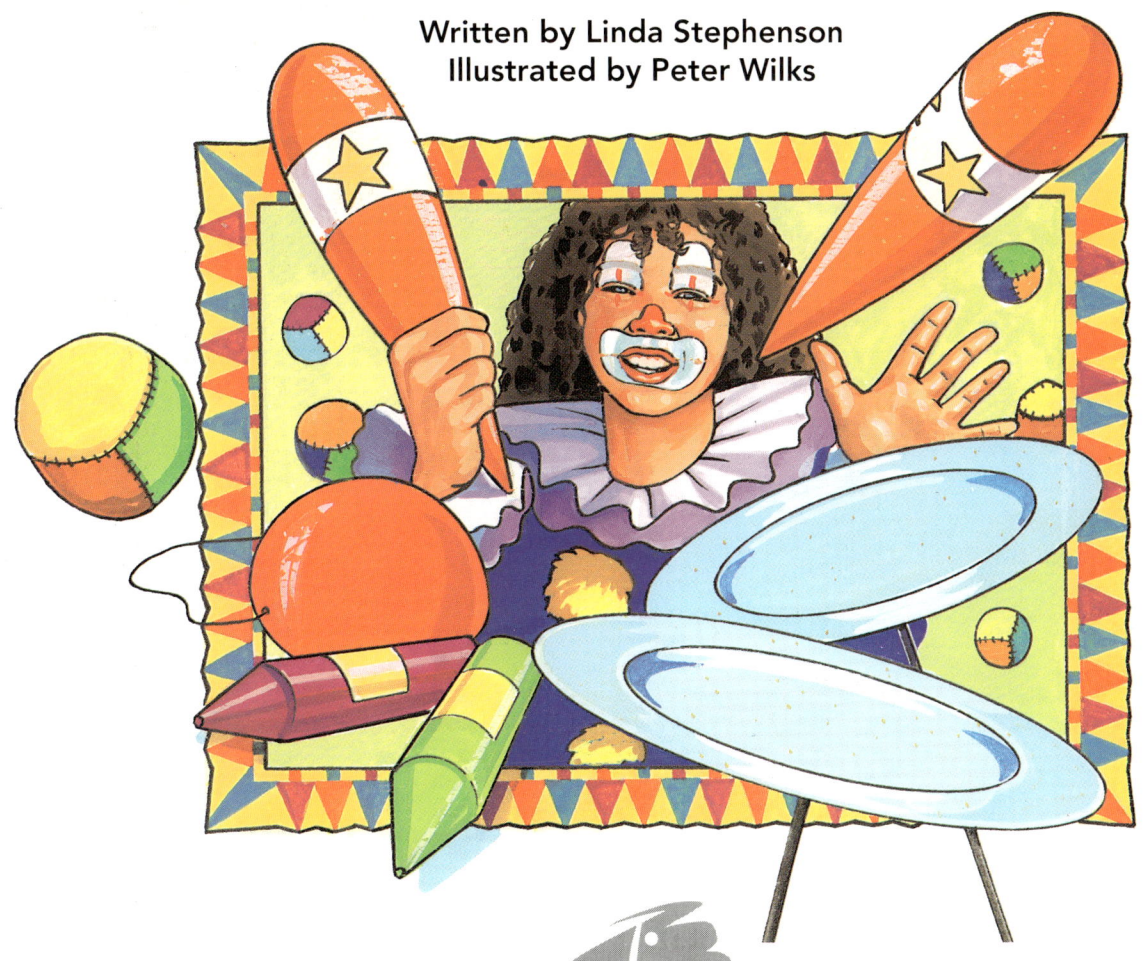

Written by Linda Stephenson
Illustrated by Peter Wilks

HENDERSON
PUBLISHING PLC
Woodbridge, Suffolk, IP12 1BY England

Getting the Juggle Bug

Hi! Welcome to New Circus! Learning to juggle may be a new hobby idea but the skill certainly isn't. It goes back centuries. Not quite to the dinosaurs, but, if they could have, they would have juggled.

Nobody really knows when it started, but records trace it back to the court of the Egyptian Pharaohs. And Socrates, that famous learned ancient Greek, told of seeing a woman juggling 12 hoops! Well, we're not going to juggle twelve of anything, or even try hoops come to that. But we are going to have a go at what is known as the Three Ball Cascade.

Interested? Good! Juggling is fun and it will give you plenty of street cred. Throwing and catching three objects with only two hands sounds impossible, doesn't it? But it's not. We're also going to try some other skills such as diabolo, devil sticks and plate spinning. But more of these later. There's heaps to do on juggling alone and a section on how to make your own beanbags.

So get cracking on all the moves in the following pages and you could end up doing this.

SCARF JUGGLING

Okay, you know what juggling is all about so let's get on with it! The easiest things to juggle with are nylon scarves. Why? Because they move so slowly, giving you lots of time to throw and catch. But remember juggling is all about throwing. If you don't throw properly, you won't catch so easily.

So let's assume you have your scarves ready. You will need three, of course. But we only start with one. A handy tip is don't do this outside or near an open window where there is a draught. Nylon scarves work so well because they are light. But one puff of wind and they will be off up the garden and you will spend all your time running after them.

Right, we're indoors, out of draughts and ready to begin. Pick up one scarf and grasp it in the middle. Use your 'best' hand. This is usually the hand you write with. Now go to the next page to see what you have to do!

One and two scarves

You're standing holding one scarf in the middle with your best hand... yes? Toss this scarf into the air across your chest and catch it with your other hand. Easy peasy huh? Now toss it back again. Still easy peasy? Do this ten times.

If things get a bit jerky and you start getting mad, stop. Put the scarf down and shake your hands and wrists for a couple of minutes. This will loosen you up.

Now take a second scarf and, leading with your 'best' hand, toss one scarf into the air. When it's reached its highest point and starts to fall, toss the other scarf. The scarves should cross over and you should catch them in opposite hands. Say to yourself 'throw-throw, catch-catch."

Difficult, eh? If you're having problems, imagine a huge X in front of you. The first scarf goes up one line of the X and the second goes up the other.

Three scarves

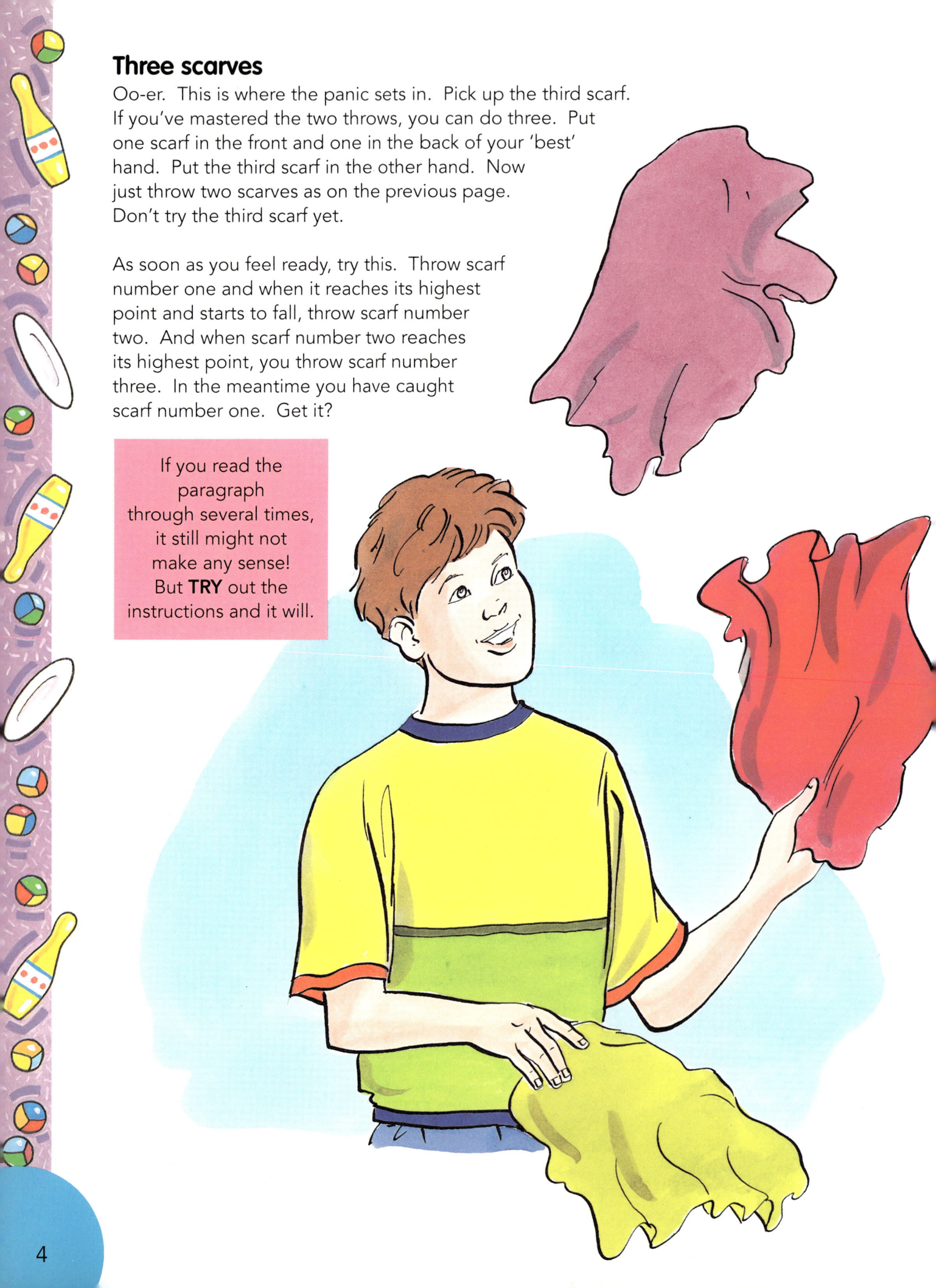

Oo-er. This is where the panic sets in. Pick up the third scarf. If you've mastered the two throws, you can do three. Put one scarf in the front and one in the back of your 'best' hand. Put the third scarf in the other hand. Now just throw two scarves as on the previous page. Don't try the third scarf yet.

As soon as you feel ready, try this. Throw scarf number one and when it reaches its highest point and starts to fall, throw scarf number two. And when scarf number two reaches its highest point, you throw scarf number three. In the meantime you have caught scarf number one. Get it?

If you read the paragraph through several times, it still might not make any sense! But **TRY** out the instructions and it will.

A simple trick

Okay, you've mastered the three scarf cascade pattern and you can juggle a bit. Practise until you can do about twenty throws in a smooth rhythm. Don't worry if you keep dropping the scarves. Keep practising and you will soon be catching nearly everything! Dropping does mean you are improving in all the circus skills, funnily enough!

Now, having impressed your mates with the fact you can actually juggle, gobsmack them with some tricks.

Place one hand with a scarf in it, on your hip and rotate the two remaining scarves clockwise in your best hand, throwing them in a circle pattern. Now try this with your weaker hand. This will be a bit harder.

Slot this into your juggling pattern and Wham! Bam! You have your very first juggling routine.

Some harder tricks

Getting good now, aren't we? Let's try some harder tricks. The first is called a Column.

The Column

Hold two scarves in your 'best' hand and one in the other. Throw a scarf from each hand straight upwards at the same time. When they reach the highest point and start to fall, throw the third scarf up the middle. Catch the two falling scarves and throw them again. Catch the middle scarf and throw again.

Good fun, eh? Repeat for as long as you want and slot into your routine!

You can also vary the paths of the scarves. Instead of two up the side and one up the middle, throw two up the middle and one up the side.

6

Under the leg!

Now for something really flash. Raise your 'best' knee (that's the one the same side as your 'best' hand!). Start juggling by throwing the scarf under your leg! Mega, huh? Next go under the leg in your juggling pattern. The secret is, as soon as you have thrown with your 'best' hand, raise your leg and make your next 'best' hand throw under the leg.

You can also throw behind your back. And, also, instead of a toss up, try blowing the odd scarf up into the pattern.

But do make sure you practise in soft, safe places as it has been known for beginners to fall over!

BEANBAG JUGGLING

The problem with scarves is you can't juggle with them outdoors, so the next objects to try are beanbags. They are heavier than scarves and move quicker so you don't have as much time to catch them. Also, they are more likely to break things in the house, so don't start beanbag juggling near light fittings, televisions or expensive ornaments or you might find this book and your beanbags confiscated by mum or dad.

Find a safe space and begin with just one beanbag. (You can make your own - see page 20.) Shake your hands and wrists first just like you did with scarf juggling. Then, keeping the bag just above head height, toss from your 'best' hand to the other hand, then back again. Keep your eyes on the highest point of the throw, not on your hands. Imagine you are in a telephone box if you like.

Two and three beanbags

You've managed to toss one bag from hand to hand. Now clap your hands in-between tossing and catching the bag. Now clap your hands twice.

Okay, let's move on to two beanbags. Remember how hard it was to toss two scarves? The pattern is the same with beanbags, but as they move quicker there is less time to think!

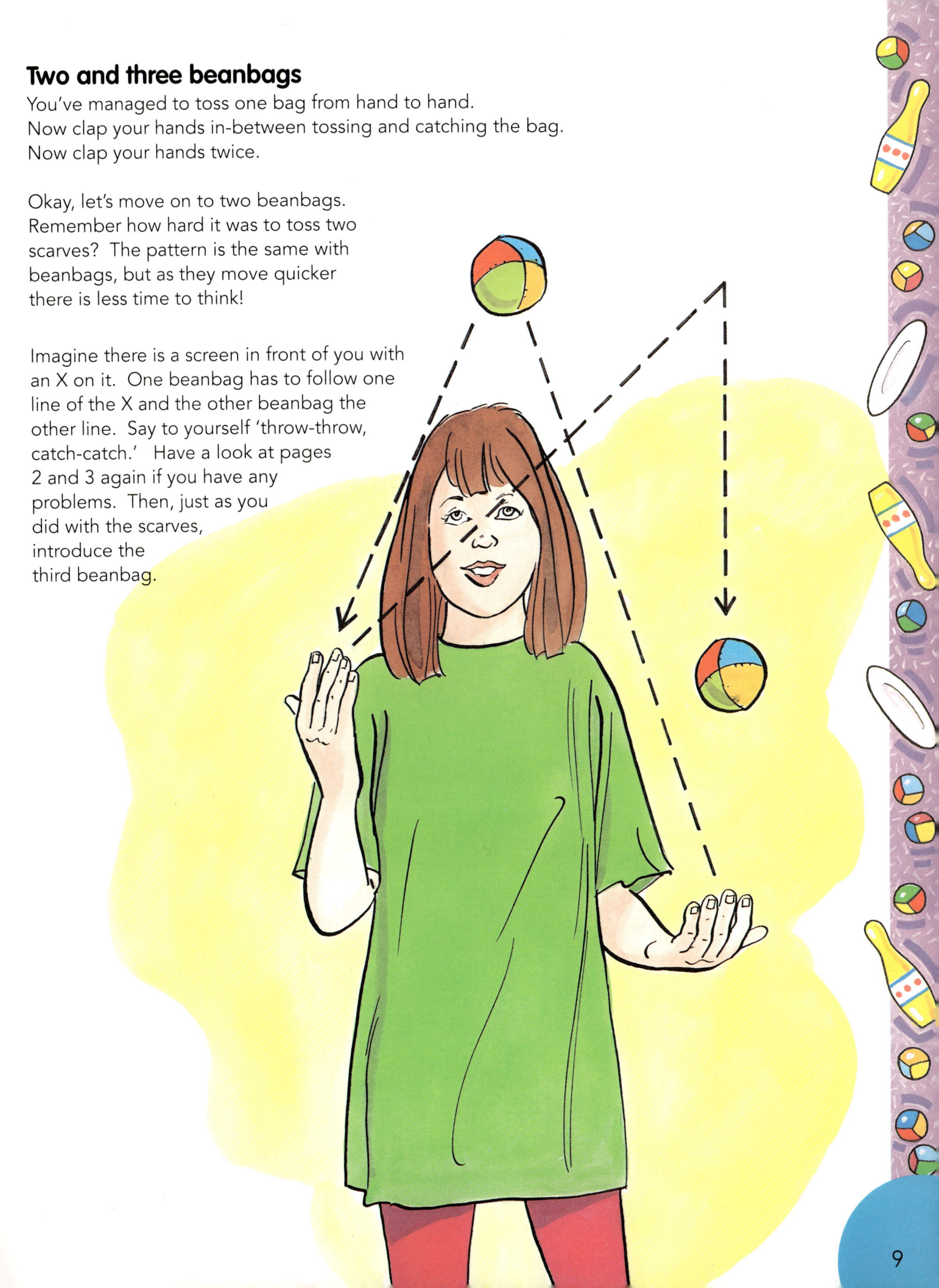

Imagine there is a screen in front of you with an X on it. One beanbag has to follow one line of the X and the other beanbag the other line. Say to yourself 'throw-throw, catch-catch.' Have a look at pages 2 and 3 again if you have any problems. Then, just as you did with the scarves, introduce the third beanbag.

Three Ball Cascade - with beanbags

Put two beanbags in your 'best' hand. Grip the back one with your little and ring finger, and hold the front one with the remaining fingers and thumb. Place the third beanbag in your other hand.

Toss the front beanbag. When it reaches its highest point and starts to fall, toss the beanbag from the other hand to make room for the first one to land. When the second beanbag reaches its highest point and starts to fall, toss the third beanbag to make room for the second one to land. Then throw the fourth beanbag. Hang about!

This is a THREE ball cascade. But the fourth beanbag is the first one second time around!

Count your throws and by the time you can do 20 throws and 20 catches you can call yourself a beanbag juggler and you are ready to go on.

How to vary the Three Ball Cascade

Before we go onto to any tricks here are some things to do with the Three Ball Cascade pattern. Try to get into a smooth rhythm and vary your height. Juggle very low, then very high, ceiling and light fittings permitting, of course. Then try very narrow and then very wide. But don't go mad and hurl the beanbags across the room.

Play some music and try and juggle in time with the beat. Also, fix your eyes on something beyond the beanbags and try to juggle by instinct. Or, maybe, talk to someone whilst you are juggling. This will help juggling become second nature to you.

If you find your throws keep moving forwards, try juggling facing a wall. You could also try juggling beside the bed, then if you drop a beanbag onto the bed you don't have to bend down so far to pick it up!

11

Some tricks

The tricks we did in the scarf juggling section can all be adapted to beanbag juggling, apart from the blowing one. Don't try that one with beanbags or you might end up with a black eye! Try this one instead. It's called the Reverse Cascade.

Reverse Cascade

Forget all about the X and think upside down U. Start by throwing one beanbag along an upside down U path in the air to your other hand. Release the beanbag at your shoulder level and catch it with your other hand about waist level.

Then, as soon as you can throw this way from hand to hand, introduce the second beanbag. Throw the first and, as it peaks, throw the second one over the top of it.

Get a smooth rhythm and go for the third beanbag. Remember as one reaches its highest point, throw the next one over the top of it. Sounds really HARD. And it is, but have a go. You can do it.

The Shower
(without getting wet!)

Some of you will have been part way to mastering this trick by doing what is known as 'playground juggling.' That is, throwing two beanbags round and round in a circle. One hand does all the throwing whilst the other does all the catching. Do this with three beanbags and you have what in juggling 'speak' is known as 'the shower'.

Here's what to do.
The secret is to throw really fast so be careful where you practise this.

Start by holding two beanbags in your 'best' hand. Throw them one at a time in a high arc but so fast that the second beanbag is on its way before the first one lands.
Do this ten times.

Now put the third beanbag into your other hand. Throw the two from your 'best' hand and just before the first one comes in to land, pass the third beanbag into your 'best' hand and throw it. That's all there is to it! Phew!

13

FLOOR JUGGLING

So far we have talked about juggling in the air. Fancy doing some juggling on the floor? I don't mean dossing on the carpet whilst you juggle - I mean bouncing balls off the floor in a juggling pattern. Obviously you will need quite a hard surface and balls that bounce well. You can buy special bouncing balls, but hard balls from pet shops also work well. Tennis balls don't, so forget about those.

Choose a suitable place like the garden path (not your bedroom floor, or the kitchen where there are mugs and glasses everywhere). Bouncing balls have a habit of finding the one thing in the room that will break, so do be careful.

Okay, we've found a suitable place and we have three hard rubber balls. Stand with your feet slightly apart and toss one ball a little way into the air with your 'best' hand and allow it to bounce across to your other hand.

Now go to the next page!

Floor juggling - two and three balls.

Practise bouncing one ball until you can do it smoothly, then go on to the second ball. Toss ball number one and allow it to bounce. Just before catching ball number one, toss ball number two to make room for the catch. Good, eh?

When you have mastered this two ball bounce, introduce the third ball. Once again, put two balls in your 'best' hand and lead off with the front one in hand that holds two. The secret, of course, is, just before you catch, you toss the next ball. It's easier than juggling in the air.

Once you have mastered this, mix the floor juggling with the air juggling. Really cool, huh?

15

Juggling with a friend

This is also known by the smart name of 'Three Ball Interchange.' You will need three plastic footballs, that's all. Size doesn't matter, but don't make them too big. And ALWAYS do this outside or in a large hall.

Stand facing each other, about a couple of metres apart. Start by passing one ball to each other so you get used to the way it moves. Then move on to passing two. Partner 1 throws the first ball and, just before catching, partner 2 throws the second ball.

If you have trouble, you may find it easier to bounce the ball to each other, instead of throwing. This will give you more time.

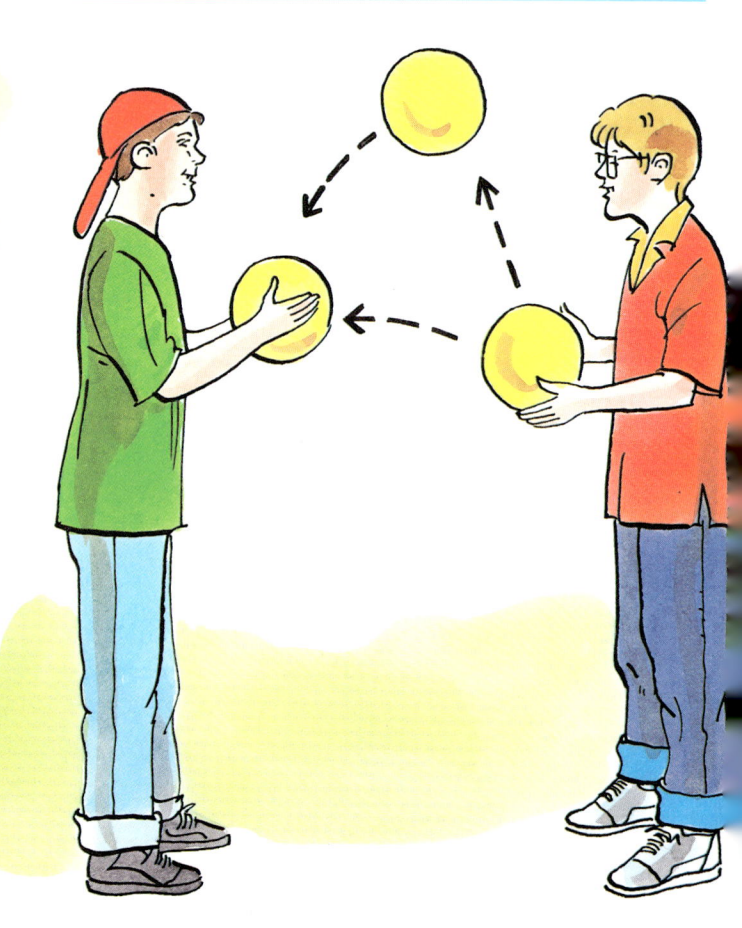

Now introduce the third ball. Partner 1 holds two whilst the third is held by partner 2. Just throw like you did with two. The secret being, just before catching, throw. Easy peasy.

Sideways passing

You've found a friend who likes juggling. Try this easy form of passing. Use beanbags for this as scarves are too 'floaty'. You will need FIVE beanbags.

Stand side by side. Partner 1 holds three beanbags and partner 2 holds two.

You are partner 1, of course. Begin to juggle the Three Ball Cascade. Count your throws and, on a number agreed by you both, throw a beanbag to partner 2.

Partner 2 then begins to juggle and, on a number agreed again, tosses the beanbag back to you.

You can keep this up as long as you like and work out a short routine, varying the number of throws. It's really good fun. Try using an egg as the object to pass, but hard-boil it first!

SIAMESE JUGGLING

I said earlier that no one really knows where juggling came from and Siam, or more appropriately Thailand, isn't the place either. Siamese Juggling is named after Siamese twins, who are joined together at birth. In juggling 'speak' Siamese Juggling is where two people juggle three beanbags between them, as if they were one person.

This is what you do.
Find a friend or a relative and stand side by side very close. You can put your arms round each other if you like. But check the other person doesn't mind first! If you are standing on the right-hand side, then you use your right hand and the other person's left hand is your left hand. Get it? You juggle normally, but use the other person's opposite hand as if it was yours!

Make your own beanbags

Right, that's as far as we go on juggling. You've plenty to get on with and here is an easy way to make your own beanbags so you won't have to spend a fortune buying some.

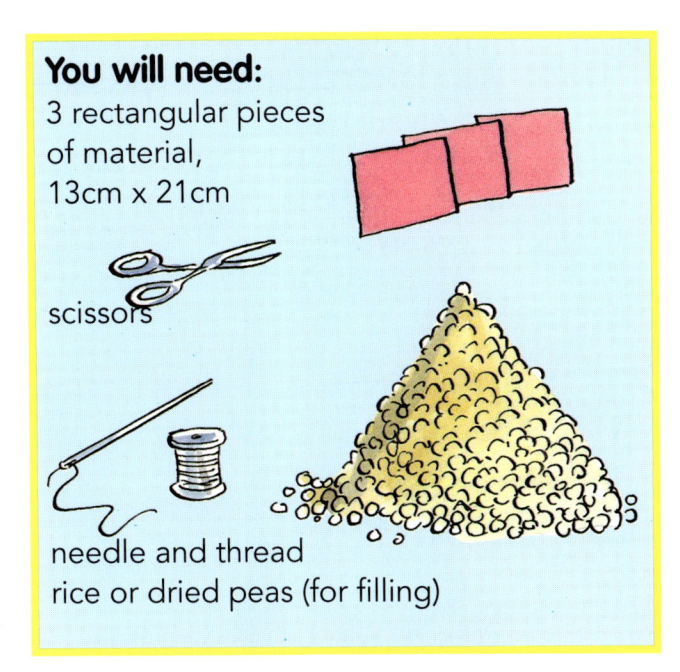

You will need:
3 rectangular pieces of material, 13cm x 21cm
scissors
needle and thread
rice or dried peas (for filling)

1 Cut out the rectangles of material - ask an adult to help you if need be.

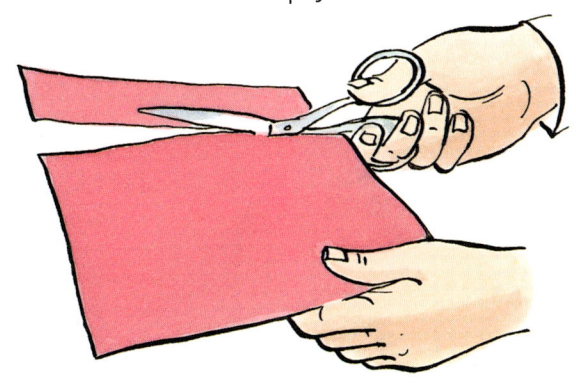

2 Fold one piece in half from A to B (see diagram).

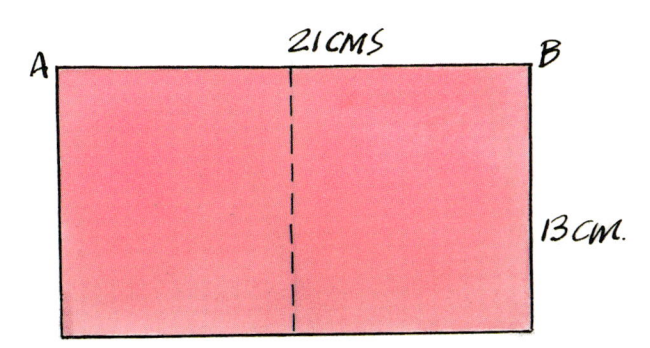

3 Stitch up the side using a very tiny hem. 5mm should do.

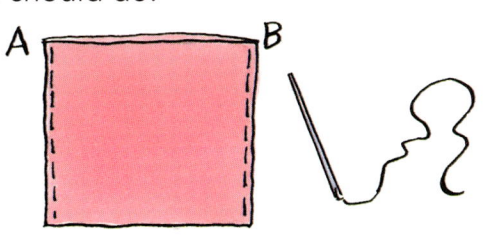

4 Turn inside out and fill with rice or dried peas.

5 Put in plenty if you want a firm beanbag. Put in a small amount if you prefer a squidgy one.

6 Now along points C and D make a small hem and stitch the beanbag together.

7 Oversew this to make it firm.

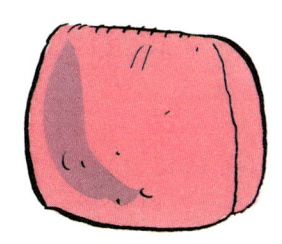

8 Repeat the action with the two other pieces of material and you have your juggling set!

THE DIABOLO

It's time for something different, now. The diabolo is a bit like a yo-yo, but it's not attached to a string. It looks like two cups bolted together in the centre. It is spun on a string tied between two sticks. Sounds boring, eh? It certainly isn't. It's really good fun!

It originally came from China and was made of bamboo and wood. It was solid and whistled or hummed when spun. The name isn't Chinese, though. It comes from classical Greek, meaning to 'throw across'. Maybe Socrates saw these in action, too.

Nowadays, diabolos are made of rubber or plastic. But they can still do a bit of damage, so only practise in places with no expensive ornaments and fittings or places where there are high ceilings. Outdoors is best with your back to the sun, provided it is shining! Be careful if is wet underfoot, as wet diabolos won't spin so well. Don't go too near the fence, either, as your diabolo might end up next door by mistake.

Unfortunately, you can't really make one yourself, but they can be bought in juggling shops or some of the larger toy stores.

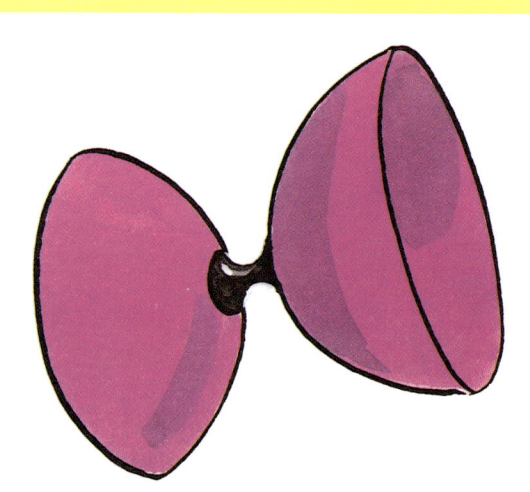

Getting the diabolo started

Choose an appropriate place to begin. Lay the diabolo in the centre of the string and place on the ground. Hold the sticks in each hand. Grip about one third of the way along and put your index finger along the line of the stick. This will give you more control.

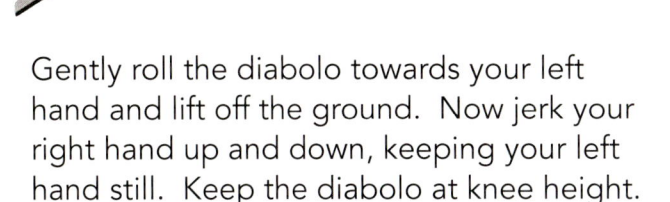

Gently roll the diabolo towards your left hand and lift off the ground. Now jerk your right hand up and down, keeping your left hand still. Keep the diabolo at knee height.

It's spinning now, isn't it? No - you're in a knot?! Hmm...try again! Get the diabolo started. Then, if it starts to turn left or right, you must turn with it. You must always face a diabolo. Now it will try to tilt either forwards or backwards. Correct this by moving your right hand in the OPPOSITE direction of the tilt. That should make the diabolo flat again.

Phew. They're clever these diabolos. They will try and control you. You must try and be their boss or you'll end up in tangled heap.

21

Getting up speed - The Whip!

One of the biggest problems when trying to do tricks with a diabolo is getting it to spin really fast. If it is spinning too slowly, the diabolo will happily knot itself in the string and drive you bananas. Diabolos love spinning fast so, to please them, first master this move called The Whip.

The Whip

In The Whip, the diabolo flies from side to side as your right hand whips across your body behind your left. Just raise your left arm, slightly, and whip your right hand under it. The diabolo will fly. It might fly right off the string if you're not careful, so mind where you do this! If the family dog or cat is watching, make sure he/she is not in the firing line.

Another simpler, but not so effective way to increase speed is to cross the sticks and rub the diabolo strings together. This will increase speed but won't wear the string out or catch fire.

The High Toss

We're now moving on to the spectacular stuff. The High Toss looks really cool, but is quite easy to do.

Choose a spot where there is room to toss in the air. Get the diabolo spinning really quickly, using one of the methods mentioned on the previous page. Hold the sticks about the width of your body apart.

When you are ready, raise and open your arms so the string tightens and the diabolo is lifted into the air. Give it some oomph, too, to help it on its way.

Catch it again by putting your string in a diagonal and catching the diabolo by the right-hand stick. It is easier to see the string here. The diabolo will slide down to the centre of the string. Don't try and catch it in the centre as it is harder to see the string there. Watch out for your front teeth, too! Try and keep the diabolo as far away from your face as possible.

23

Variations on The High Toss

Once you have cracked tossing and catching, here's some more things to try:

Are you any good at skipping? If so, give the diabolo a toss and try a quick skip over the string before you catch it. Have a practice first with the sticks and string to make sure you can skip with it. It might not be long enough. And you don't want the diabolo crashing down on you whilst you untangle your feet, do you? Try and work it in with the toss.

Then, try keeping the string taut after tossing the diabolo and let it bounce up and down on the string like a trampoline.

Thirdly, instead of tossing straight up into the air, try tossing the diabolo in a circle shape from left to right. It's just a variation, but it can look good in a routine.

A couple of easy stunts

The first one is called Around the World - and it won't take 80 days to perfect. Simple trick this one, but it does look good. Here's what you do:

Around the World

Get the diabolo spinning very fast, then hold the two sticks close together and swing the diabolo in a complete circle.
Immediately swing it back again. Good, eh?

Now try a cross-over. This is easy, too. Get the diabolo spinning very fast, toss into the air and catch with your arms crossed. Throw it again and catch in the normal way. Good stunt for the routine.

Over the leg this time

When we started showing off our juggling skills, we tossed under the leg. We're now going to show off our diabolo technique and toss over the leg.

Get the diabolo spinning really quickly using the whip action. Move it down the far right-hand end of the string near the stick and raise the left leg over the remaining length of string. Then, when you are ready, aim for the string the other side of the leg and toss. Wah! It's gone over and you've caught it. Well, you might need a few goes to perfect it so, like The Whip, make sure no one is in the firing line.

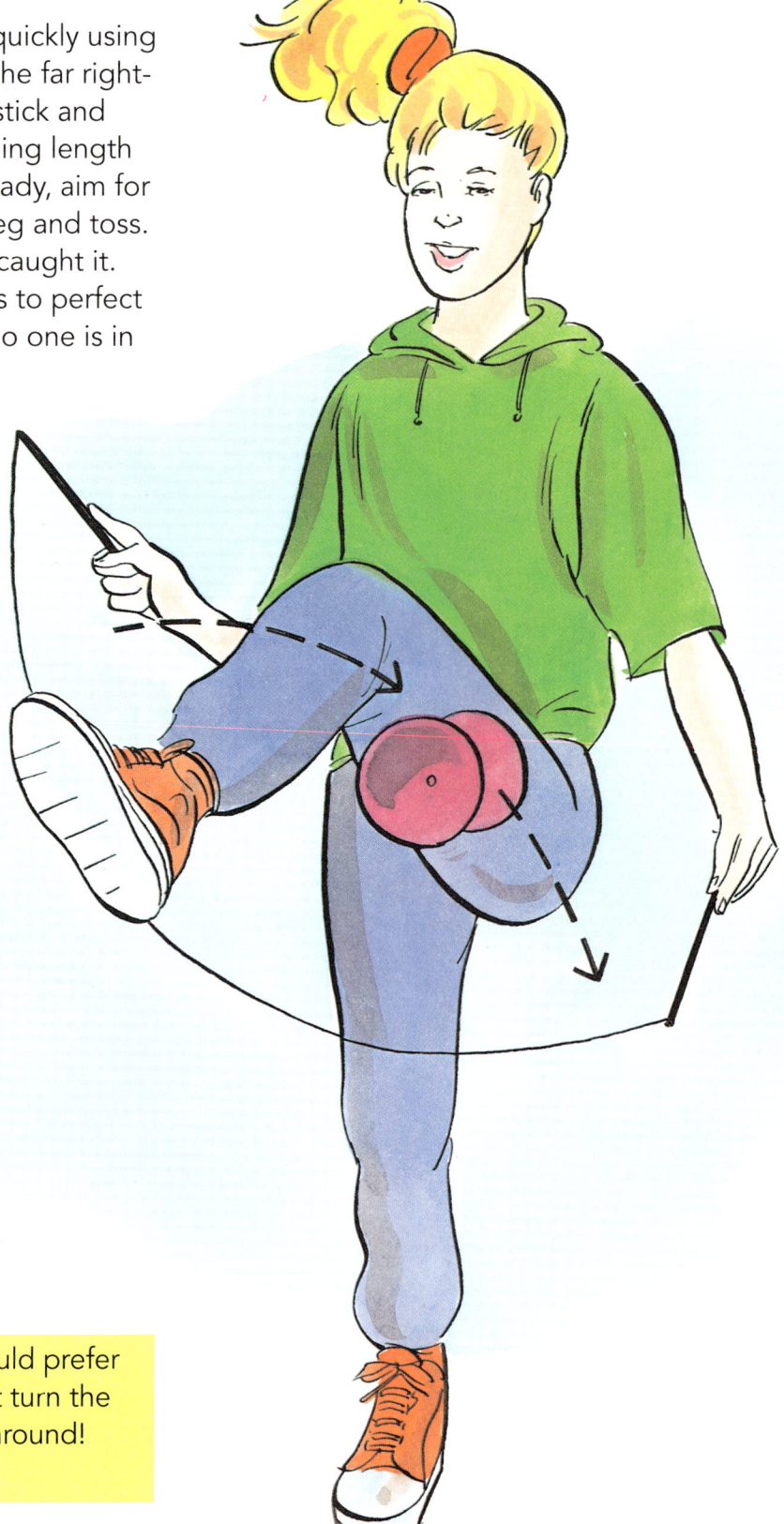

> If you are left-handed and would prefer to toss over the right leg, just turn the instructions the other way around! Easy peasy.

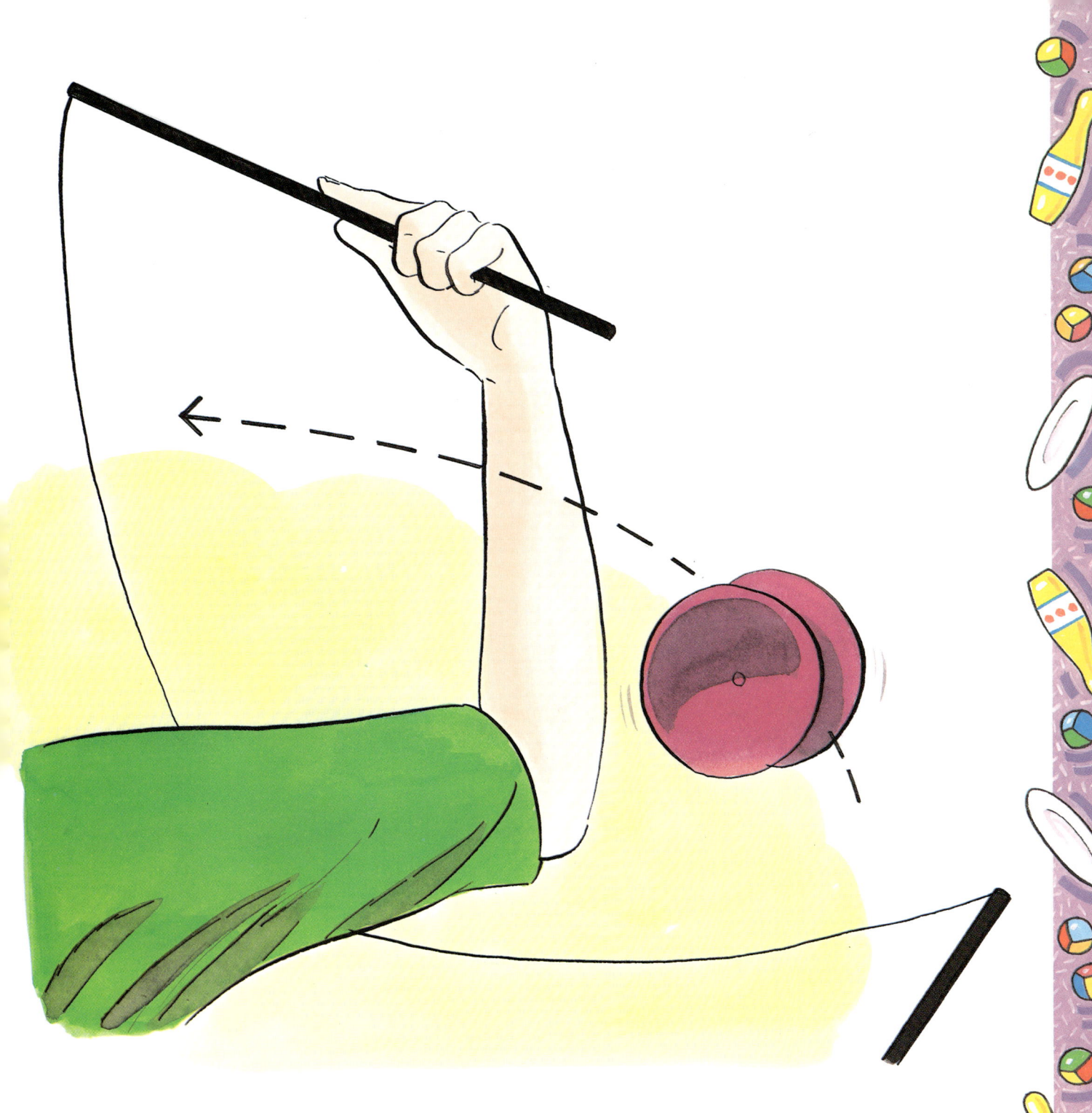

Over the Arm

This is a mite harder than over the leg, but don't let that put you off.

Get the diabolo spinning really quickly and allow it to spin right down the far right-hand side, just as you did with the over-leg toss. Now bend your left arm backwards and pass the string under your arm about half way between your shoulder and elbow. Raise your left arm so the string is visible. Now raise your right hand, aim for the string the other side of your left arm and toss the diabolo over.

Whoops! Bet you missed first time, as this trick isn't easy, but keep going. You'll do it in the end!

27

The Monkey Climb

What have monkeys got to do with a diabolo? The answer is nothing, unless they are making a monkey out of you! It's just a name to describe a trick. It's a hard trick, too, and will take a fair bit of practice. Here is what you do.

Get the diabolo spinning very quickly, then, using the right-hand stick, loop the string around the centre of the diabolo. Raise your left-hand stick upwards and very gently pull down on the right-hand stick. The diabolo might hurtle up the string and lock itself onto the left-hand stick to start with. But, with practice, you will be able to get the diabolo to climb slowly up the string, hence the name!

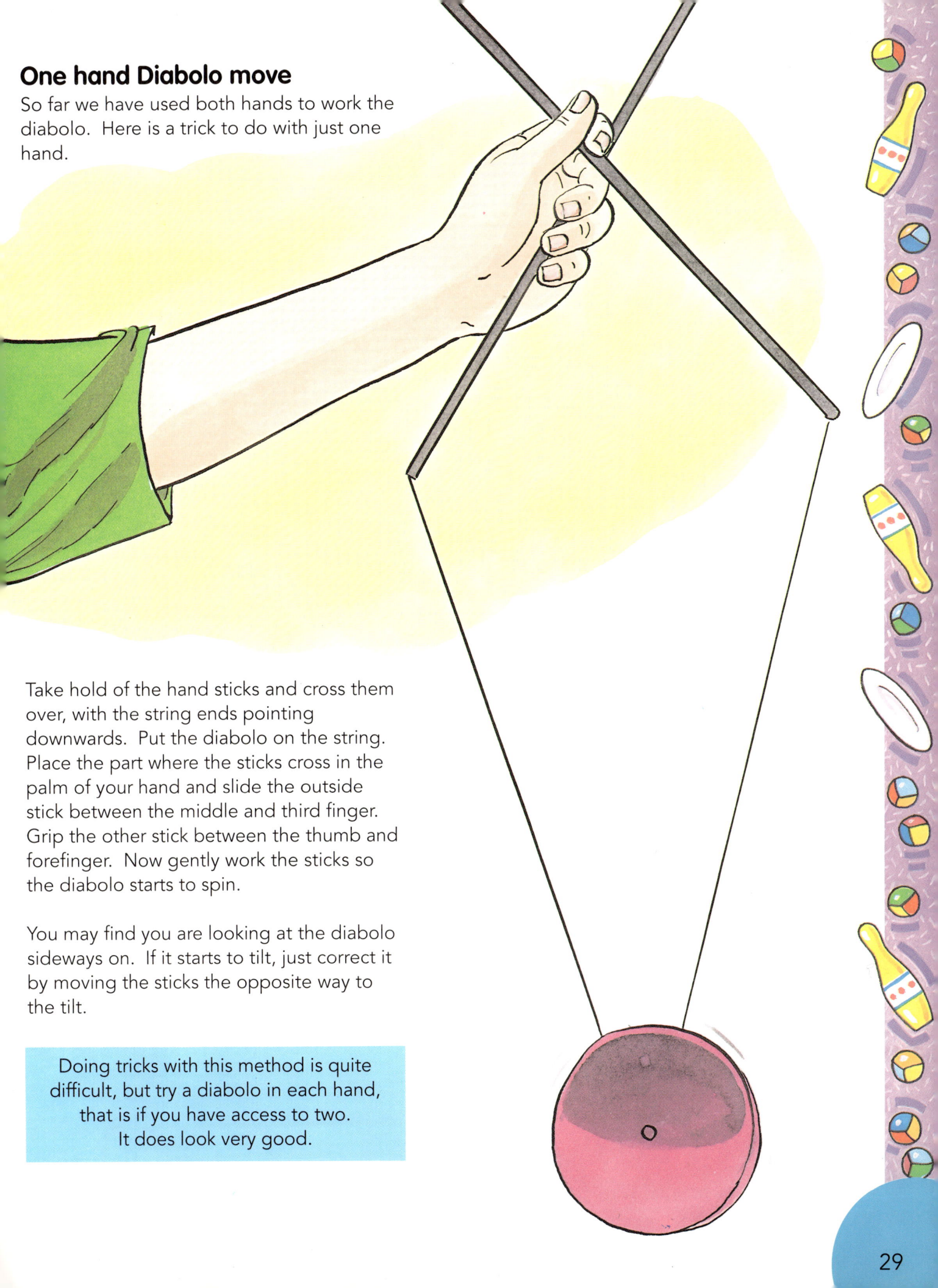

One hand Diabolo move

So far we have used both hands to work the diabolo. Here is a trick to do with just one hand.

Take hold of the hand sticks and cross them over, with the string ends pointing downwards. Put the diabolo on the string. Place the part where the sticks cross in the palm of your hand and slide the outside stick between the middle and third finger. Grip the other stick between the thumb and forefinger. Now gently work the sticks so the diabolo starts to spin.

You may find you are looking at the diabolo sideways on. If it starts to tilt, just correct it by moving the sticks the opposite way to the tilt.

Doing tricks with this method is quite difficult, but try a diabolo in each hand, that is if you have access to two. It does look very good.

Diabolo Tennis

You borrowed a diabolo from a friend for the last part of the one hand diabolo spin. So now try some diabolo tennis with that friend. This is really good fun.

Start by using one diabolo. Stand side by side, facing the same way about a couple of metres apart. Choose a large space for this. Outdoors is best, although a hall with a high ceiling would do. Don't do this in the house. If one of you is left-handed, you will have to stand side by side but face opposite ways.

Get the diabolo spinning really quickly, then, when you feel ready, toss it to your partner. Partner should catch it using a diagonally held string, then toss it back. Easy peasy, eh?

When you have mastered this, try using two diabolos. One goes high and one goes low or there will be some pretty frequent midair collisions!

THE DEVIL STICK

That's the diabolo over. Now we'll move on to something really hard. (Only kidding.)

You will be able to amaze your friends by seeming to defy the laws of gravity and keep a stick in the air by hitting it with two smaller sticks. There are no strings involved, or magnets, only your skill!

The Devil stick came from China and is related to the diabolo. It looks like a stretched out diabolo with no strings. It was originally called a Flower stick and was weighted at each end with flowers and pieces of material. It became known as a Devil stick in the Middle Ages. Some say because it was also called a diabolo. Or, maybe, it was thought the stick stayed in the air with the devil's help. They were very superstitious in the Middle Ages!

Devil sticks can be bought from juggling shops, or you can make your own. You can practise this anywhere, except the bath. Devil sticks don't work when they are wet! Don't do it in places where there are expensive fittings, either. Devils have been known to fly!

Getting started - a new meaning to tick-tock

Begin by holding the hand sticks in each hand about one third of the way along. Run your index finger along the side of the stick too. This will give you more control. Place the Devil stick on the ground between the two hand sticks. Always keep the sticks parallel and horizontal, about the width of your body apart. Okay so far?

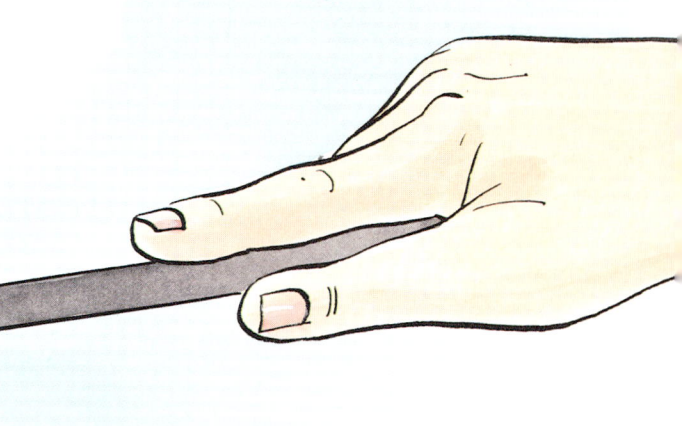

Your contact point on the Devil stick is about a third of the way down the top part of the stick. Gently tap the devil in upward movements with, first, one hand stick, then the other, so it falls from side to side. It is more of a toss-and-catch than a hit. Let your body sway with it.

Then, when you are ready, flick the devil off the ground with your best hand onto your weaker hand, then return. You are now in the air. Wow!

Tick-tock explained

So what's all this 'tick-tock' then? In Devil stick 'speak', 'tick-tock' is the sound the devil makes as it falls from side to side and hits the sticks. To maintain a steady 'tick-tock', your left and right hands must do the same amount of work. If not, the stick will go off balance and fly all over the place.

To start with, you may find yourself going very fast and may be hitting straight rather than up. Try and get a toss-and-catch feeling.

You toss from one hand stick, catch on the other and toss back. The devil should also swing from side to side, like the pendulum of clock, and follow an arc between 10 and 2 on the clock face.

By the time you have mastered 'tick-tock', the devil should have a floating appearance giving rise to comments like "it's done by magnets" or "it's on a string". At this point you can drop it just to prove is your skill!

Some simple tricks

Don't try these until you are happy with your 'tick-tock'. It must be smooth and you must be in control of your Devil stick. Devils, like diabolos, have a will of their own. But with this skill, the aim is to be smooth rather than to go fast.

Right, you're ready. Try this trick. As you toss the stick across with your best hand, instead of catching with your weaker hand, let the stick spin around the stick and then toss back. Now repeat this action but spin the stick over the best hand stick. Really cool.

Now try a 360° flip. Start by balancing the Devil stick on your best hand stick. Now flip it over so it does a full turn before you catch it on the weaker hand stick. Try this the other way, from weak hand stick to best hand stick. Now work this into your 'tick-tock'.

Double sticking

Double sticking, or 'trapping' as it is known, is where you hit the Devil stick with both hand sticks at the same time. One stick is above the centre of the stick and the other below. Your contact points are about halfway between the ends and the centre of the devil.

Start with the Devil stick on the ground. You have to alternate your hands, of course. The hand stick trapping the falling devil must be in the higher position. Once you have gained your rhythm, take off and try it in the air. It will drive you mad to start with, but it is fun and another variation.

35

Toss and (maybe!) Cross

Hold the two hand sticks horizontally in front of you. Now lay the Devil stick on top. Gently bounce the devil up and down. Then, when you are ready, give it a flip so it does a half turn before you catch it again on both sticks. Get used to doing this. Then give it some 'oomph' - flip the devil around in a full 360° turn and catch again on the two hand sticks.

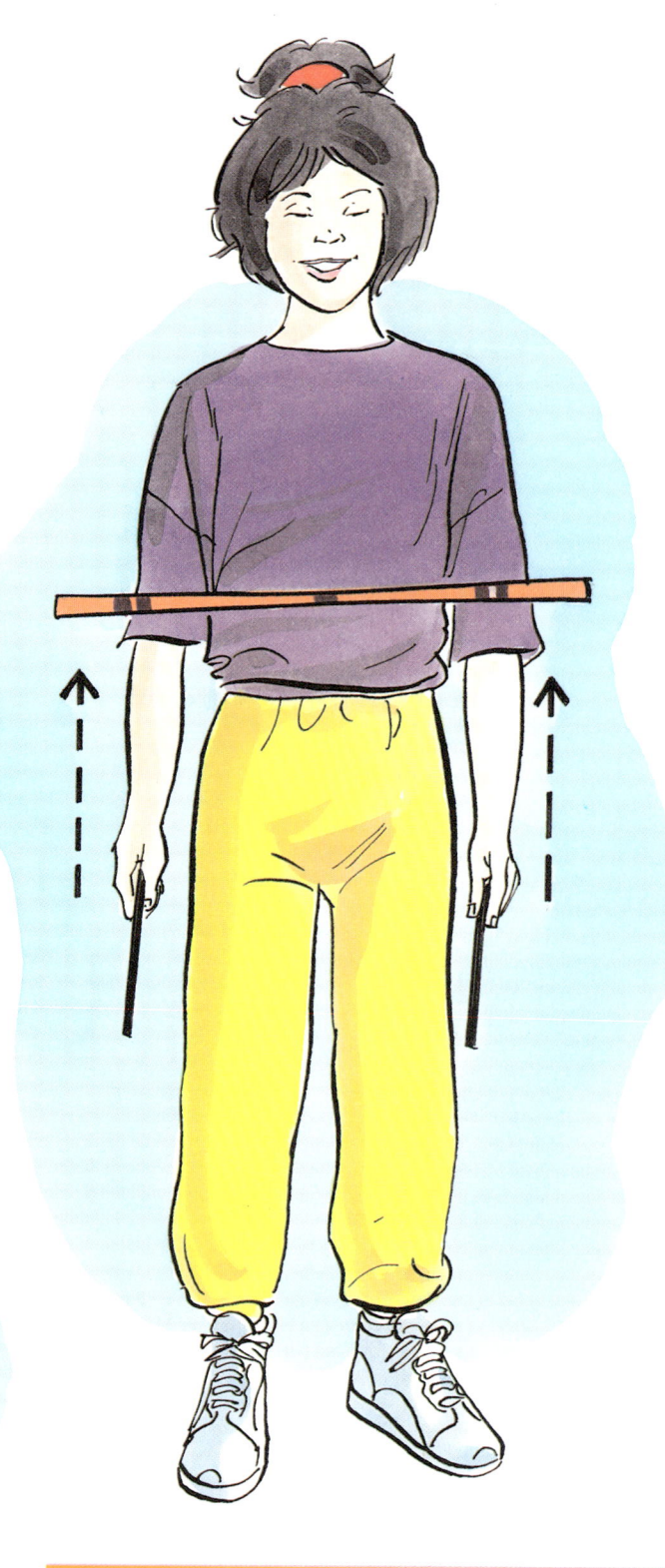

Now for the 'cross' bit. Toss the devil into the air and cross your hands before catching on the sticks. Toss again and uncross your hands.

Devil stick with a friend

You remember we played diabolo tennis? Well, you can do a similar move with the Devil stick. You will need a friend, of course, and two sets of hand sticks. One Devil stick will do.

Stand facing each other, about one metre apart. Partner one starts off a 'tick-tock' and then, when ready, says "Now" and tosses the devil onto the best hand stick of partner two. Partner two does the 'tick-tock' (and any fiddly bits) then passes back to partner one's best hand stick and so on.

You can also do Siamese Devil sticking. Two people share two hand sticks and one Devil stick, just the same as in Siamese Juggling (see page 18).

Make your own Devil stick

Right, we've read a fair bit about what to do, so here's a method of making your own Devil stick.

You will need:
3 lengths of 12mm dowelling (2 x 48cm, 1 x 70cm - you may need an adult to help you cut the wood to the correct size)

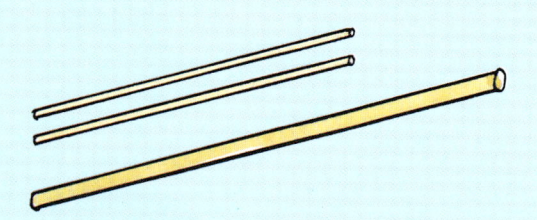

2 rolls of handlebar tape (available from cycle shops)

a roll of insulation tape (although you won't use it all)

6 coins (about the size of 2 pence pieces - you can either use 2 pence pieces or similar sized foreign coins)

1 Once the wood is cut, you start work on the biggest stick. This is going to be the actual Devil stick.

2 Begin by taping three of the 2 pence pieces to one end of the stick using the insulation tape.

3 Pile them one of top of the other and pass the tape over and round until they are quite secure. Do the same with the other end of the stick.

4 Cover the rest of the stick with handlebar tape until all the wood is covered.

5 Lay the stick on one finger somewhere near the middle of the stick. When you find the point where it will balance on your finger without falling off, mark this with insulation tape. You may need to experiment to find the right spot.

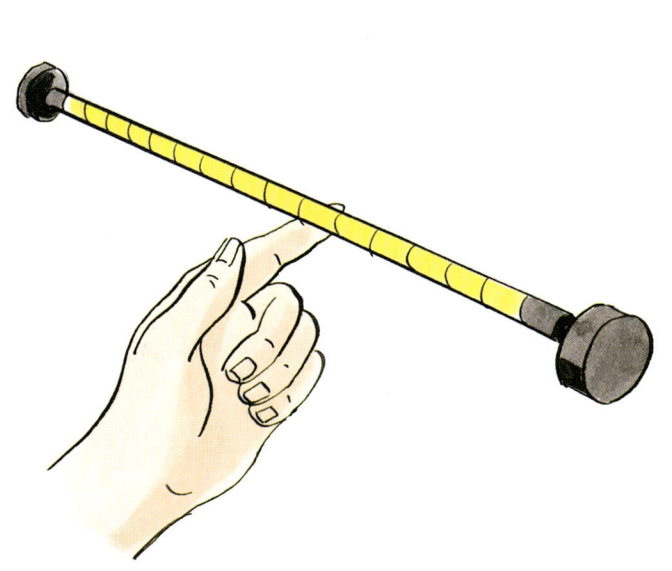

6 Now mark the quarter marks on the stick. You can measure these if you like or guess them. This is just for decoration.

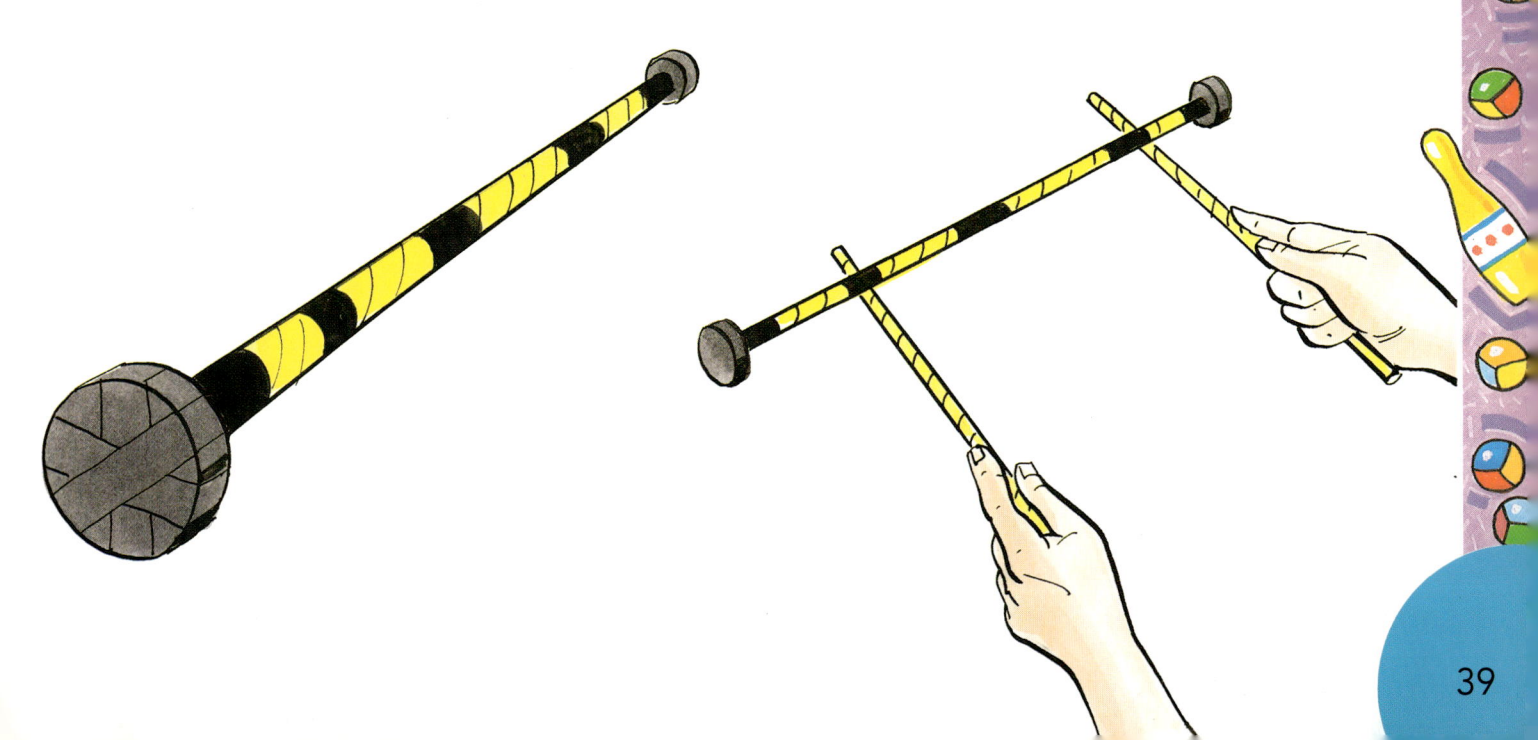

7 Cover the other two sticks in handlebar tape. You've probably guessed these are the hand sticks.

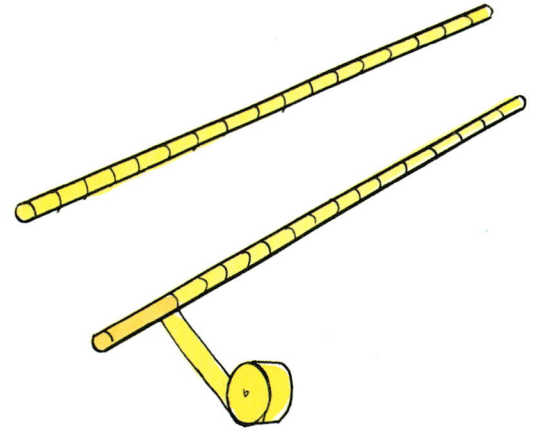

You are now ready to try out your homemade devil. You may like to cover the devil again in more handlebar tape or even insulation tape. Don't put insulation tape on the hand sticks. If you do have problems, it is possible to buy hand sticks separately, quite cheaply, from juggling shops.

PLATE SPINNING

Here we are at the final skill. Plate spinning comes from China, yet again, and is as old as the hills. It came to Europe in the Middle Ages and was performed at mediaeval banquets. When we say 'plate spinning', that doesn't mean spinning china plates. Special plastic ones are used, as the crash factor involved in learning and performing with them is so high you would smash more plates than on a Greek night at a restaurant. So don't try this with mum's best dinner service. You can buy the spinning plates from juggling shops. You can also make your own (more about that later).

Old hats spin quite well, too, provided they are flat-ish. But do make sure the owner doesn't intend wearing it again.

Choose a place to do this skill out of wind and draughts. They work best indoors, away from expensive fittings and the family pets. But you can spin outside, provided it isn't too windy.

Getting into a spin

Okay, you have a spinning plate and a stick to spin it on! Choose a suitable place and check the dog or cat is well out of sight. They should have got the message by now, anyway! Underneath the plate you will find a wide rim. On the end of the stick you will find a sharp point. Put this sharp end inside the rim of the plate. Take hold of the stick by the other end and run your forefinger along the side of it. Hold the stick up in the air. The plate should be hanging by its rim. Yes? Good. Now we'll move on.

Keeping the stick very straight, start rotating your wrist round in a circle. The plate will start to spin. Move it faster and faster and, gradually, the stick will move to the centre of the plate where there is a specially designed groove. The plate should now be spinning on its own, so stop rotating your wrist. Make sure your stick remains straight. If it isn't, the plate won't spin properly.

If you have problems getting going this way, just cheat and put the plate straight onto the stick and give it a quick spin with your hand! But the spin is not so effective.

41

Some finger spins

Right, you have the plate spinning speedily on the end of your stick. Now put your left forefinger (or whatever is your weaker hand) into the groove, take the stick away and place somewhere safe. Then, hey presto! the plate is spinning on your finger.

Curl the plate around your left arm. Now pass it around your back and pass it onto the forefinger of your other hand. Raise your right knee and pass under your right leg from the outside to the inside. Pass the plate back to your left hand, pick up your stick and toss the plate back onto the point.

Phew... that was a neat routine, all in one paragraph!

Tricky sticking

Here are some tricks to do with the plate and the stick.

Get the plate spinning quite quickly and do a gentle toss, just a few inches at first. Keep the stick very straight and catch the plate again on the stick. Try tossing a little bit higher now.

Next, find a plate-spinning friend and do a throw-and-catch routine. Toss the plate to your friend. Your friend should catch it on his or her stick and then toss it back to you. Stand quite close together at first, but move further apart as you get used to the skill.

Now, once you have the plate spinning well, turn your best hand upside down and grasp the centre of the stick. It might feel funny, but when you are ready, toss the plate, turn the stick round the other way and catch the plate on the blunt end (really cool trick, this one). Reverse the action to get the plate back on the sharp end.

43

Mega balances

Astound your friends by doing something that looks really difficult, but is actually quite easy.

Get the plate spinning and then put the blunt end of the stick in the palm of your hand. Let go. Does it fall over? No! It won't if you keep your eye on the plate and not your hand. It might help to move your hand a bit to keep the balance, but it does look good.

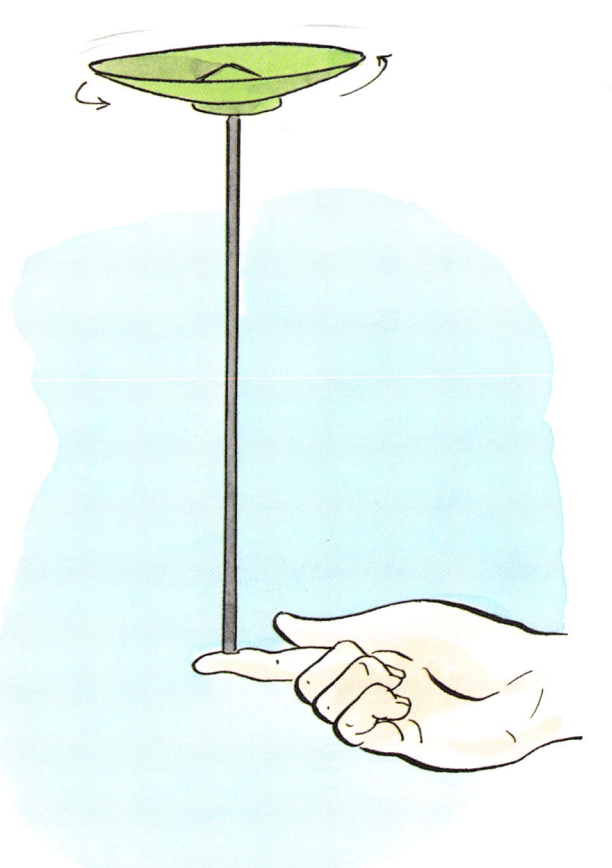

Now try the same trick with the plate stick balancing on the end of your finger. Once again, keep your eyes on the plate and don't look at your hands. It will balance.

If you have any large feathers, try balancing those on your hands. Keep your gaze on the top of the feather.
Word of warning - don't take things that aren't yours to use!

Sticky curling

On page 42 we did some great curls with the plate spinning on our fingers. You can also do curling with plate spinning on the stick. It is similar but different!!

Start by getting the plate spinning very quickly. Then, lift your best leg (the one the same side as your best hand) and pass the stick underneath from outside to inside. Take hold of the stick with your other hand. Now pass the stick and plate under your other leg from outside to inside and take hold of the stick again in your best hand. This is different to working with the plate on your finger as the sticks are much longer and you will have to lift your leg much higher. If you have problems, practise with just the stick in the first place.

You can also curl the plate and stick around your arms and pass behind your back, This is, more or less, the same as with the plate spinning on the finger.

THE BIG FINALE ...
Multiple Spins!

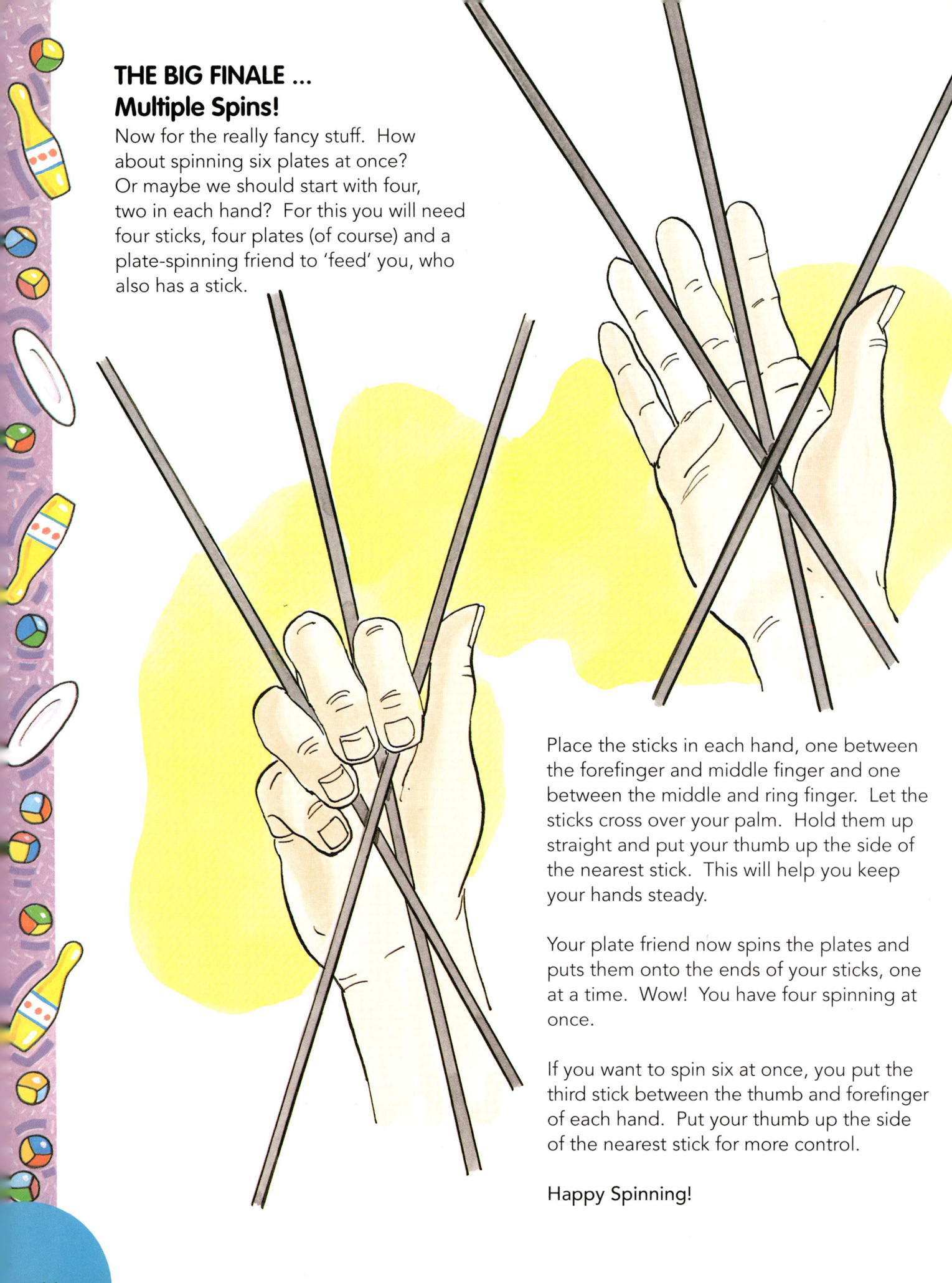

Now for the really fancy stuff. How about spinning six plates at once? Or maybe we should start with four, two in each hand? For this you will need four sticks, four plates (of course) and a plate-spinning friend to 'feed' you, who also has a stick.

Place the sticks in each hand, one between the forefinger and middle finger and one between the middle and ring finger. Let the sticks cross over your palm. Hold them up straight and put your thumb up the side of the nearest stick. This will help you keep your hands steady.

Your plate friend now spins the plates and puts them onto the ends of your sticks, one at a time. Wow! You have four spinning at once.

If you want to spin six at once, you put the third stick between the thumb and forefinger of each hand. Put your thumb up the side of the nearest stick for more control.

Happy Spinning!

Make your own plate

Although spinning plates are very cheap to buy from juggling shops, you can make your own out of paper plates bought from the supermarket.

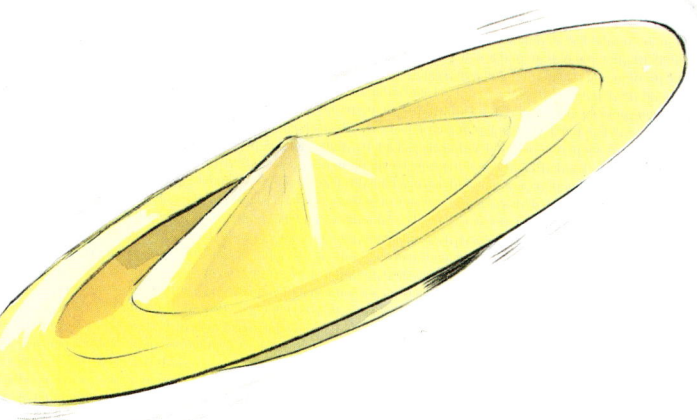

You will need:

3 paper plates, 23cm across

1 paper fruit bowl, 18cm across

glue

sticky tape   scissors

80cm length of dowelling, or a big pencil

With your pencil, make a small hole in the centre of the bottom plate. Do not let the hole go through all the plates.

Cut the base out of the bowl and glue the remaining piece onto the bottom of the plates to make the deep rim. Reinforce with sticky tape if you need to. This rim must be quite secure.

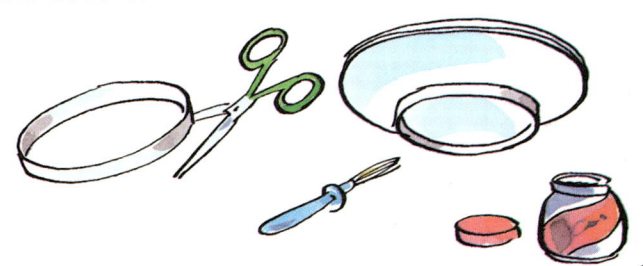

Sharpen your large pencil or, better still, 80cm length of dowelling, and you are away!

Turn the plates wrong-side up and fold them into two and then four. Make sure the folds match and that they cross in the centre. Unfold the plates and stick them together with the glue, one on top of the other.

47

GET THE SHOW ON THE ROAD
Stage a juggling show to impress folk with your new skills! Any time and any place when people get together could be an excuse for doing a show.

Short and sweet
15 mins. is the longest your show should be - shorter if possible.

Variety is the spice
Don't choose five tricks of the same sort. Warm up with the Three Ball Cascade (a short, instantly impressive trick), then follow it with a more complicated move. Towards the end of your act, rope in a member of your audience (preferably one who can juggle!) and involve them in a duo trick. Crack jokes throughout the show to distract the audience from the fact that you are having to concentrate. Perform a few tricks in time with some dramatic music.

Rehearse!
Your audience will get fidgety - not to mention unappreciative - if they have to sit around for too long between tricks. Keep your act tight and plan it so that one trick flows naturally into the next. Have some prepared 'patter' connecting them all. If you do have to keep people hanging around whilst you set up for the next stunt, chat to them, in a jokey way, about what you are doing. This will keep them interested.

The Incredible Ivy Juglin!
To add to the fun of a one-person variety show, invent strange names for each trick and use posters showing these names to announce the moves. Put specially prepared posters on an easel, in the right order, and pull each one off to show the next trick. Wear a different get-up for each set of tricks. You don't need elaborate costumes - it would take too long for you to change and your audience would get restless. Don a different hat for each of your acts. A simple false moustache and beard with no explanation will keep your spectators guessing and giggling throughout. Wear an outlandish wig and dress and mime to an old record. Keep costumes simple and uncluttered - you don't want droopy sleeves to interfere with your juggling.